Wrinkles in Time and in Love

Wrinkles in Time and in Love

Poems by

Nancy Jo Allen

Cover design by Shay Culligan

ISBN: 978-1-954353-05-3

Kelsay Books
502 South 1040 East, A-119
American Fork, Utah, 84003

This collection of poems is dedicated to those who inspired them through the good and bad times in my life, but especially my husband Terry who has changed my life in ways immeasurable.

Acknowledgments

The author is grateful to Marta Ferguson for her carefully considered advice, and the editors of the following journals where these poems first appeared, some in earlier versions.

Dime Show Review: "Planting Poppies"

Firewords: "A Tattered Matchbook"

I-70 Review: "Bubbles, Patches and Wheels"

*82 Review: "Sunday Morning Newspaper"

Third Wednesday: "Art"

Volume One: "Maturity"

Well Versed: "Wedding Announcement," "Out of the Mouths of Babes," "Exit," "If I could Whistle," "Nocturne," "Paring it Down," "Castle," "From Here to Eternity," "Hiding the Chick," "Alzheimer's Stole His Personality," "I have Become Autumn," "Attic Memories"

Contents

IV

I

Out of the Mouths of Babes

For my estranged daughter

You were always an artist.
You saw what others
refused to see.

On the wall hangs a picture
you created with colored crayons
when you were but seven years old.
It is neatly divided into two meridians.
On the left, a smiling couple walks together
with hands so tightly entwined
that they appear to be an extension
of the leash they hold.
At the end of the leash tugs a small dog
pulling them through a grove of trees
so tall that you drew white clouds
high in their leafed branches.
It is marked *Reality*.
The other meridian is marked *Fantasy*.
A smiling woman,
who has sprouted wings,
floats high above one lonely,
empty chair.
She pushes a yellow baby carriage
with orange hood and wheels
set against a clear, cloudless, blue sky;
her hands grasp a smooth carriage handle:
inside is a tiny baby.

I remember when you asked me
if I would bear your children.
The thought of carrying and delivering
a child frightened you.
Was it the pain, or the commitment?

13

We two spoke of intimate things
in soft, low tones.
Things that I never spoke of with your sister,
your aunt, your grandmother.
I always thought that you
could see inside me. See my
sadness like branches covered
in icy layers of snow. That, somehow, you knew.

One day, you taped a carefully scissored
poem to the inside of my computer cabinet door,
where your father would not see.
It was about what a woman should have,
what a woman should know.
It included knowing how to break up,
knowing how to live alone,
knowing who she can trust,
and knowing what she can accomplish.
Did you know the extent of my pain?

At first, it was powder and lipstick
on his collars. Then his very flesh
smelled of perfume. He claimed
it was his aftershave.
He hadn't shaved since his early twenties.
And there was the painful twisting of my wrists
when we were learning conflict resolution
at your middle-school.
I used words. He could not.
He was quite proud, in the end,
that he had not hit me.

He could not speak to me,
but he did to others when I refused to stay.
He so desperately did not want
the truth to be known
that he created a fantasy from reality.
A scenario in which I starred as the betraying wife.
I foolishly chose to ignore it. Why hurt you?
Children need fathers—even fantasy fathers.

You are a part of me:
beating heart,
vulnerable flesh,
fragile mind.

You precociously knew a woman
like me wants to believe the fantasy.
She accepts man's seed.
She cultivates her womb.
She harvests the fruit.
She protects the children
in chariots that launch them
to soaring heights.

Quadratic Equation

With many notes
penciled amid the graffiti
on my Algebra book's
brown-bag cover
which sat on my desk
during quizzes and tests,
I passed with a D-.

I still cannot grasp quadratic
equations and am not proud
of cheating to pass.
I am the x
in your life's math.

As your mother, though, I
do not see myself as unknown.
The values of your logical expressions
are unknowns to me:
not numbers, but people.

Your $a, b,$ and c represent
voices that to you are not zero
and are therefore solvable,
yet your problem remains unsolved.
This reminds me of a blue plastic ball
you pushed shapes through with pudgy
fingers. This early encounter with math
did not work without the appropriate shape
to pass through the matching hole.

Graph your equation anew
with the appropriate factors
of one for you and one for me
and let's see where the x and the y
actually intersect on your life's graph,
for I have value, and so do you.

In Retrospect

From the shelter of our covered porch,
I look across the grass and gardens
at an amorphous mass.
Under the hackberry's branches
lie two featherless hatchlings
shaken loose from their home.
This may be the very family
that doggedly constructed
nest after nest
under the eaves
atop the downspout curve
above our BBQ.

They built. I destroyed.
Shelter for them there
was inconvenient for me
in our outdoor kitchen.
I recall the determination
with which the mates
returned again and again.

With mud-filled beaks
they built the foundation,
and moved on to frame
the home, unable to line the nest.
I stepped through the door
and pulled down the grasses.
I felt I was doing them a favor
when I spread cooking oil
and chili pepper on the spout
having no shared language

to reason with these robins,
I chose to communicate
the impracticality to them.
Finally, they chose the hackberry
branches in squirrel territory:
less safe, and more exposed.

As I take in the scene at my feet,
I think of my daughter's two
ectopic pregnancies
that ended in loss,
and wonder about the new pregnancy
on this her due date.

Han

There is no literal English translation. It's a state of mind.
Of soul, really. A sadness so deep no tears will come.
And yet there's hope.

—President Bartlet, The West Wing

My fingers caress the folds
of satin fabric, beadwork,
and tiny covered buttons
that line the back of the dress
from the neck
to the fitted waistline.
The train is still buttoned
after nearly thirty-eight years.

Recently,
I heard of women who
collect wedding dresses
to make into burial clothes
for stillborn babies.
It seems a reasonable
choice to make,

for the gown
will not be worn by my daughter.
She has wed,
and cut me from the whole cloth
of her life.
I am dead to her
without knowing why.

The newspaper
reports a fifteen-year-old boy
stowed away in an airplane wheel well
flying from San Jose to Hawaii.
His family had lied that his mother
was killed by a rocket
half a world away in Mogadishu.
He learned she was not dead.

This child survived
the acrid smell
of jet fuel,
its bitter taste,
the deafening sound
of roaring engines,
altitudes of thirty-eight-thousand feet,
and temperatures
as low as eighty-five degrees
below zero to reunite
with his mother.

Wedding Announcement

It was only five months
before your wedding
that I learned of your engagement.
Under duress,
you phoned me,
and it was clear you
had no intention of inviting me.
No intention of my meeting
your future spouse—the man
who would take the baton
from your father's arm
at the altar. That I
would not be welcome
to button your dress,
tell you about sexuality,
disagreements,
reconciliations,
or attempts to alter the past,
the present,
the future.

You mentioned
with hot head,
sharp tongue,
and icy veins,
that I had somehow
wronged you citing
events as brief as a poem
on a page.
Clearly you found meaning
in those moments that I
could not see.

Just five months
before exchanging vows,
rings,
tossing flowers,
tasting roasted beef,
hearing toasts made
with the sweet bouquet of wine,
and kissing
when glasses sounded
by the clappers of silver spoons,
you spoke
of your failed college romance,
ten years past.
You claimed
that I had wanted you
to marry him back then.

You were nonplussed
when I stated that was not
my choice to make.
What you had failed to hear
from my lips that day so long ago
was a completed thought.
Had you listened,
you would have known
I offered to bind your heart
like a bandage
is meant to bind gaping flesh,
for your heart was broken.

You would have learned
I married your father
on the rebound.
Beware.

That was all I wanted to tell you.
My observations must have pierced
like a sword,
but they were thrust only
as the sun thrusts its rays
and casts light
onto a darkened path.

Divorce is the sum of all its parts,
not just selections chosen as if
from a box of broken glass.
At birth, we are not given a map.
We wander twisting paths
navigating with the palms
of our hands,
or the tips of our fingers,
along dark corridors,
and are blinded and deaf
as we try to speak no evil.

I chose to speak no evil
about your father, for the truth
would have stolen from you
a very important person in your life.
What would have been gained
by slicing you in two?
Who would have
walked you down the aisle?
Who would have danced
with you?

I see now that my silence
stole another important person
from your life,
yet your buttons were secured,
but not by my fingers.

II

Exit

You have begun to fade,
glowing red in the sun's reflection
off my 4x4's paint.
Now it's mine—
mechanical failings and all.
No need to belabor memories,
so I plan to sell it and the house.
That's when we will really settle.
For now, it's more like removing chains
from tires that slip in snow. The divorce
just minutes new—final.

Outside the courthouse,
you rap on my Chevy's window
expecting the glass to glide open.

I depress the control on the door,
the window slips between the panels.
You stand a few feet from my face:
I in the driver seat, you a pedestrian.
You make a dramatic statement.
Nonplussed I shrug my shoulders,
electronically raise the glass,
peering through it—no longer a fish
in a bowl—knowing this time
when I park in the garage,
I will not gasp for air,
but will emerge erect as early human
from primordial soup.

A Tattered Matchbook

props up the table leg
in the restaurant's back corner.
It is worn from the mop
sopping up accumulated dirt
night after night. It is a popular table
for couples who need propping up
during a marriage,
before a divorce,
or after coming home
to an empty dining table
for the first time in years.

A woman cups her chin,
cocks her head and stares
at her first proper date in thirty years.
She is cut loose like fish from line.
She chooses the proper utensil
with the precision of a props
manager hidden behind velvet drapes
who keeps the story on stage
moving along for an audience.

This time around she knows
what underpinning she needs
to build upon, what colonnade
to choose to avoid becoming
an empty vase like a prop
on some man's stage
thrown by a deceitful lover,
or like that matchbook
near her shoe under a heavy leg
in a dark corner.

Sunday Morning Newspaper

Coffee spills on the business
section, edges toward the blue
velvet box on the countertop
as I read about *Gray Divorce*
and financial distress.

The box cushions a diamond
bracelet worn once—worth ten times
what the pawn shop will pay.

I pour more coffee
and turn the page.

Castle

Flames burned, sparks floated,
cardboard curls rose in swirls
from the trash burner as dad
poked castle ruins into the can.
I knew I could not keep it forever.

I had biked to the grocery store,
searched piles of boxes—
for the right one—
balanced my bicycle with care
to not scratch cars parked along the streets,
and navigated potholes
created by Minnesota ice melt.

The castle had it all: crenelated battlements,
stairs, turrets, gated drawbridge, a moat,
stabled horses of varied colors of molded plastic
in tiny poses from passive gentility
to stately rearing, and seven dwarfs
guarded Snow White in her castle.

I spray-painted it gray, hand-painted blocks
to evoke medieval stonecutter's precision.
Easter grass covered the perimeter
between the painted blue moat
and the castle walls. A section of green
plastic strawberry basket became the gate
at the cod-fish box lid drawbridge.

It seemed an impenetrable fortress,
yet one match laid siege to the battlements
sending smoke and ash
into the blue Minneapolis skies

much like my marriage would years later
burn by a match lit by the hand
of another woman.

Red Buds and Bonsai

Like Degas' ballerinas in repose,
red buds line the streets.
Some fold in upon themselves,
others form groups
intertwined,
delicate,
lovely.
The buds have opened red
to shades of pink dressing the trees
in airy crinoline tutus.

Each displays unique beauty
unlike the countenance of oak,
linden, maple—so predictable—
and show like Japanese bonsai
trees on a large scale.

This wabi-sabi aesthetic evolved—
from nothingness—
by controlling roots,
confining the plants
in small spaces, thwarting growth,
and bending them to the will of another's vision
of beauty for meditation.
In desperate times they fold in
upon themselves
like women.

Empty Vessels

common
to the sea
not land
bony beauties
now crowded
in revealing
glass jar
delicate
whorls
spires
in shades of
brown
white to black
translucent silver
polished
by waves

we too
are consumed
growing hard
in limited
color range
once as
bivalves
connected by muscle
we grew
pearl children
now we are
separate
empty vessels
you and I

Art

keeps odd hours,
so must the artist
who wakens
in darkness
answering the call

as it gnaws like mice
consuming crumbs
of emotion,
of memory,
and ropes
that bind
the lion's strength.

Like an Alluvial Fan

the sediment of my life's river
spreads out creating rich soil
in which to root,
to sprout branches
and leaves and color.

Amid, Behind, and Silent

For Christine Blasey-Ford
and all hysterical women

Amid cold, carved stones
set one atop another,
covered with lichen
of yesteryear,
offset for strength
and stacked together
against her

she exists.

Behind wrought-iron bars
she grabs for something
always just out of reach.
She stands frozen.

Wrapped in gauze to bind
wounds: she bleeds.
Her words are primal
against raging storms
and tagged *hysterical,*
yet they are as real
as a hand over her mouth,
as true and silent as snow
falling on tears.

Survivor

You do not have to be a silent victim
adrift on a sea of grief.
You do not have to choke
on the miasma of lavender smoke
that settles over the burnt forest
of your subconscious.
You only have to let the cloud of fog
lift after March snows rain on the wind
in the earliest hours outside
the window like a photograph
in black and in white.

You do not have to let the memory
march along the shore
of your sea of pain.
You do not have to listen to the voice
in the attic of your memory
after it lays you in ruins.
You only have to let the linens
hung in the farthest corner of your cellar
warm you like a shawl
as you sit among the ruins
within, holding your breath
in the wild stillness of memory.

You do not have to wall out the latest light
during your dying days' end.
You do not have to cloud the nearest
presence in fog, and in rain, and in ruin.
You only have to lift the coffin lid,
and reveal the holy truth
that you were unjustly wronged,
then walk away.

III

At the Zoo

behind bars and glass the animals
are as tame as a stuffed menagerie
on a child's bed resting
and ready to spring to life
in a small head with a large imagination.

Then one rises, stretches, yawns
a cavernous mouth, or swings limb
to limb ululating a language
known only to others of its kind.
Acrobatic infants to geriatrics
on a porch live in one large encasement.

In the corner behind this glazing
in this circus show
sits a grandmother chimp.
She slowly lowers her sagging body
to meet the zookeeper
who carries a small bag of trinkets.
The woman on the safe side of the barrier
removes items of curiosity for the primate
to view just out of her reach.

Suddenly, this powerful world of nature
captured like a snow globe reflects
what it is to come for all who
roam the earth long enough.

Cemetery

The sky reflects her thoughts:
it is blue and clear. Clouds
float along like soft memories
edged yellow with the color
of passing time where stories
gather together in graves.

An airplane flies to a new
destination dropping shadows
on numbered marble markers
in lettered sections on snowy ground
like coach seating inside the fuselage.

The plane fights gravity
as do the souls here.
Faith lifts believers who dream
of a better place beyond
life's beauty and pain
that will shape into something new
to which nostalgia
can never truly return us
until pain becomes secondary.
Then, every day is a beautiful dream
wrapped in eternity.

She smiles.

Planting Poppies

I open a mouth
in the early morning earth,
and remove a bedding
plant with care
from its fragile,
plastic container
that protects roots
as tangled as veins
that feed human
bodies. I ponder opioids
that this beautiful plant
provides to terminal
patients. The plant
grows in fields
soaking in sun rays
like bodies on beaches
converting sunshine
to something useful;
narcotics act upon networks
of nerves, quieting pain
screaming for attention.
My hands close soil
in place and Gaia
swallows roots. I
think of Mother's lips
closing around that last pill
pressed under her tongue.

Spanish Moss

Memories drape like Spanish moss
in lacy and airy spaces
hanging from curved branches
of her once sturdy,
oaken brain,
but what she wants
is heavy lead that cannot blow in the wind,
but set firm like a doorstop
letting small to large recollections
enter her mind—
solid as headstones
in a groomed graveyard.

Broken Stringer

She resurrects friends long gone
nodding in recognition
to her unseen guests
now spilling like beads
falling from a broken stringer—
and she sweeps her hands in waves
as she sleeps collecting each precious gem
should they roll under furniture,
or fall into cracks in the floor
lost forever amid dust and dirt
losing all luster.

Attic Memories

Like half-shaded windows
peering into the attic of her soul
she tries to recreate happier times
when life was a sturdy
steel-framed bed
warm as hand-stitched quilting
and safe as plush toys,

but, in truth,
time has left its mold and dust,
cracked her walls,
peeled her paint,
grimed her glassy panes
like a mirror on a chifforobe
that reflects deep sadness,
or a candle in need of a match
to flicker light on a somber truth,
like priscilla curtains
that droop from rods
blocking light
like the way she often felt
after making love—
a caved ceiling
and strewn rubble.

Alzheimer's Stole His Personality

Once, he shared his dislike
for the other lady living in their home
telling his wife of forty years
that this woman was *bossy.*
She did not tell him
there was no other woman.

He repeated himself often,
and some relatives grew uncomfortable
as his stares into space and his drools grew longer.

When it became too much for her
to care for him at home,
their son helped find an open bed
at a nursing home. His remaining days
were brief, and he died
in a bitter Minnesota January.

When the time came to walk
away from the coffin,
after the parish priest's request
for perpetual light
to shine upon his soul,
and a twenty-one-gun salute
honored his service to the country,
she wailed in heated pain, *No!*

Amid swirling snow that covered icy
ruts along the driveway path,
family supported her
to the waiting black car
with the red, white, and blue
Stars and Stripes folded under her arm
held close to her heart—ready to frame.

She can still hear the sound
of frozen Holy Water
sprinkled from an aspergillum
upon his coffin like the tinkle of gravel
kicked up from tires along the road taking him home.

If I Could Whistle

Ships, trains, bullets all whistle—
cars have *bells and whistles.*
A whistle begins and ends a factory
worker's day. If he is happy, he whistles
while he works. A referee begins and ends
a sports game with a whistle
as well as cries foul during a game.
Fire departments whistle to announce calls for help.
Whistling in the dark is a pessimistic act
with optimistic hope. Lifeguards
blow the whistle on bad behavior
in a pool, or warn of danger in the sea.
Men whistle at women and some women
take umbrage while some are validated—
it's in the ear of the beholder.

My tea kettle can whistle. Birds whistle
by instinct —not reason—to call lovers.
Bing Crosby's whistle was smooth as silk.
Mother washed me clean as a whistle.
Once I blew the whistle
on a former employer—that was satisfying,
and the closest to whistling I may ever come.

Gabriel blows the whistle of a horn
gathering the dead. If I could whistle,
I would stick my fingers in my mouth
and blow like Dad did to call the dog,
but I would sit by the kitchen window
and wait for Dad to appear—not the dog.

Bubbles, Patches and Wheels

There's something about the length
of exposed arm when a man's shirtsleeve
is rolled up that gains my attention.
There's bone and sinew,
tanned skin and soft hair,
hard knuckles wrapped around a screwdriver,
pounding a nail, or tightening a vice—
repairing things. It's manly, I guess,
and I see my father working
in the basement of the home he
built when Mother was pregnant with me.
I remember learning at his elbow
how to patch a bicycle inner tube.
He would fill the laundry tub
with water, pump air into the tube,
then submerse it turning it until bubbles
of air escaped. Father marked the spot,
dried the area and cut a piece of patching.
When it was repaired, he fit it into the tire,
placed it on the rim, attached it to the bike
and began inflating. He had to reset the chain,
so he greased it while he was at it.
I then mounted the bicycle and took flight down the alley
to my next adventure much like the day
Mother and Father saw me off at the airport
for my first solo escape across the Atlantic.
It was years later Father shared heroic truths
of sortie bombing raids over Europe
from Italy to Germany. I recall his haunted face
of memories best left to rot in brain-fold graves.

Now, in my old age, I wonder what stirred
inside him that day as wheels up I headed to Spain.
Did he sit encased in a bubble of glass
with a machine gun rattling his hands
as Axis powers battled Allies in patched planes
of the 451st B-17 squads wanting safe wheels down?

Shrapnel

It took decades
to work itself to the surface
of his thigh.
A remnant of his last sortie
in early April 1945—
the one that sent him home
to North Dakota.
The one in which he
nearly bailed over Italian fields
far below in a parachute
he later learned was also pierced.

The shrapnel, a piece of that silk
and the Purple Heart he earned for that mission
decorate my office wall nestled safely
inside a shadow box of memorabilia.

But the box cannot hold the passing sound
of my father's voice fading like all shadows
on a cloudy day.

Scratching the Surface

Song of My Ancestors

The Irish Rail puffs and clicks steadily north
after my adventure of climbing stairs,
then hanging upside down
to kiss the Blarney Stone.
From Cork though Limerick, Clare,
Galway, and on to Mayo
where a relation named Bridget Trench
testified to the Church in 1879 that she—
along with others from Knock—
had seen the Virgin Mary, Saints Joseph and John
for the better part of an hour
as she prayed the rosary in awe
after kissing the feet of Mary
and pondered how it was like kissing air.

Out the window, on the right,
the vista stretches out for miles:
lush, green undergrowth
dotted with stone fences, sheep,
crops, and fields of peat.
Cottages whitewashed and thatched
with red lacquered doors
line gravel paths like garden flowers.
A rooster and chickens
scratch the surface for feed
that fattens them for frying pans,
stewing pots, and Sunday's painted porcelain
plates set before the parish priest.

On the left of the tracks,
vast waters of the North Atlantic
crash and scrub the shores and cliffs
cutting deep and steep. Fishing boats
dot the cold green-gray waves
like the field stones to the east of the tracks.

Here, my ancestors worked the land,
sheered the sheep, husbanded the animals,
harvested the crops, fished the sea
for the once abundant whiting and cod,
and cut the peat that smoked in curls
from fireplaces that fried their fish
and warmed their bones.
They were milliners fashioning hats
for Sunday Mass to funeral wakes.
They were doctors and nurses
who tended the sick
and kept the circle of life turning.

Villagers scratched the earth
to feed their families. Then, Mother Nature
brought blight and famine,
and headstones dotted the land,
so my ancestors packed up their stories,
religion, broken backs but unbroken spirits,
kissed the air, and boarded ships for Ellis Island.

IV

A Corpse Flower

is about to bloom at the arboretum.
The plant draws pollinators
with the odor of rotting flesh,
but your flesh was incinerated to prevent rot.
How diverse are the workings of nature and man.

We once talked of the Galapagos Islands'
diversity and beauty: as unique as Yellowstone.
Land and water filled with crabs, iguanas,
sea tortoises, blue-footed boobies,
Galapagos penguins, and the air
filled with great frigatebirds, and albatrosses.

You wished for my happiness
in love: to lose my albatross.
Red signals flash through the glass doors
beyond my balcony. Traffic
is stalled as I have been for ten years.
Denuded branches,
stretch out like my bare arms
in a moment of ecstasy
moving forward with him,
and the light turns green.

Wading in Deep

It is raining on the streets
and on the passing cars
outside my bedroom window.
I turn my face to capture splashes
of sound, and I imagine lapping waves,
sun-dappled white crests, a fish
rising from the depths of the lake,
hooked with lake weed: a green wig.

I think of you and the auburn
wig lying in curled waves upon my
shoulders. I feel my breasts
heave with waves of pleasure
your hands bring as they caress me
like breaking waves upon my shore.
You partake of my gift
imbibing your fill. The waves
continue to break in natural rhythm.

My thoughts turn to a fishing boat
outfitted with silvery minnows
in a bucket hanging on a stringer
overboard. I feel the silvery cloth
of my lingerie
as it glides over my thighs,
my rounded hips, my quivering sides,
my embossed nipples, and off over my
outstretched arms. You cast it overboard
to the floor to join a school
of unbuttoned cotton and open flies.

I remember the day you told me
you had taken up fly-fishing.
I asked to join you sometime.
I pictured wading in deep, casting a line
with silvery bait; the line stretched to its length,
jerking to a quieted halt,
and floating in the running water
as a fish glides toward the bait.

At Rest

Moonlight brightens
the edge of your cheek.
I see the gentle curves
that lead north to your ear,
and south
to your resting lips.
Your eyes,
now closed shades
in darkness: un-glowing.
Your nostrils barely flare
with hushed movement
of air in and out:
rhythmic.
There is such a gentle
and cherubic look
to your face
when I stroke it
that I feel I must
know your mother's admiration
as she watched you sleep
in her arms
upon your birth.

One Time

I left for good one time,
but came back.

He said he'd be true
to me, and I waited

for proof as years passed
along with many women.

I came back when he
wrote to tell me

he had made many mistakes.
It had taken him years to learn
I was not one of them.

Sort of melted my heart.
The best way to return

is by invitation
        with an apology.

I was true to him always
and now, I hope

he will be true to me
        always.

Ganges Means Wise Friend

Your hand,
gentle on my waist,
guides your warmth
close, cupping our bodies
like an open parenthesis
about to make a statement
left unsaid.
Your breath murmurs warm
on my neck translating
to *I love you.*
You have brought candlelight
to my gloaming dreams,
and I realize in night's dark,
death could never extinguish
this light.

I dream my body furnaced to dust
floating up chimney,
escaping earth's gravity,
chasing the soul
already rising to the heavens.
One ash catches a down draft
and is sucked into a passing car's air filter
to be discarded in city landfill:
forgotten and buried.
Another lands in fertile garden soil
becoming the fabric of red tomato
months later consumed,
sprinkled with sugar, dripping juice
down grizzled gardener's chin.
But another, drafts high over land
and sea to India where it settles
onto a shallow clay dish
lighted by oil and wick

floating in the Ganges
where sins are remitted
reclaiming order
for my disordered ashes.

You shift your body,
and I breathe in rhythm with you.

Nocturne

Ice tumbles into the freezer tray
in the kitchen. The house
moans as the northwest corner

settles onto the foundation
and the shower head
drips just one *plop.*

Conditioned air hums,
sinking softly atop quilts
that cover our bodies

entwined where we
warm one another. You
sleep—deaf ear up.

A truck rumbles past
on the highway to the north,
while wind chimes

tinkle their tympani
in sweet night air
thick and dark as molasses.

You add to this larghetto
as you breathe
purring steady notes—

I am here.

I am here.

We are here.

Midnight Blues

The clock glows blue,
the numbers blear
in my aging eyes
as time ticks forward,
silent as our bedroom:
my arms empty,
but for your abandoned pillow.
I recall your desire for me
in the night, wanting to touch,
to be touched in warm glow
was our thrill. I want your body
to block that blue glow
from my view—to loom over me again.
To desire me again. To make time
stop ticking forward awhile
as I caress not your pillow,
but your warm flesh.

Hunting

I sit in the waiting room
watching the TV mounted on the wall—
the sound is off on National Geographic.
A lioness prowls through savanna grasses
the color of her coat as she crouches,
becoming as small as she can with shoulder
blades jutting up as she lowers her body
deeper to the dirt readying herself
to capture the family's meal.

I recall when I was a young girl at play
in the neighbor's unmown lawn.
It had gone to seed and was like that
savanna grass. I pretended to be a lioness
prowling for prey to feed my family.
To care for them.
        To protect them.

A nurse enters the room
calling my husband's name.
I gather my things
and sling them over my shoulder
as we cautiously walk to the exam room
hunting for answers.

I Have Become Autumn

I am spring's reflection
of clumsy green shoots
pushing through soil
demanding notice.
I am summer's heated souls
longing to taste fruit forbidden.
I now consider what is to come.
What it is to return to infancy
demanding notice,
but unable to taste that fruit.
Autumn is living without reservation:
living with knowledge
stored like acorns in a hollow tree
to be consumed or forgotten—
to sprout or rot.
It is the last flash of brilliant
color. It precedes snow
gentle on the branch.

From Here to Eternity

She daydreams of waves
rolling rhythms
along a sandy beach.
She strolls its long-curved edge—
feet skirt dead vegetation
thrust from the water's depth.
She stops, raises her hands
protecting her sensitive eyes
from harsh sun as she searches
the vast horizon for *his* spirit.
They never had a honeymoon
in life, so they agreed in death
to seek water and sand like Lancaster
and Kerr and embrace in cool,
wet sand filling themselves
amid the swells of water
and ecstatic waves of love.

The garden hose spills water
over the top of the can
shifting her focuses to a yellow
butterfly with black spots
that drinks from pooled water
on a curled leaf of bugleweed.
The plants soak up the moisture,
regaining their shape and color.
She scans the garden's winding
scalloped edge—its shape like
lapping waters along a beach.

Wrinkles in Time and in Love

Biocentrism meets Shakespeare

Time is not cast in a die—
it is flexible.
Wrinkles are produced through
satellite travel,
distance and gravitational pull
accelerate time, altitude
from the Earth's center distorts time,
the Sagnac effect slows and speeds time
through rotation, equatorial spin—
like crack-the-whip on ice skates—
makes time run faster, and elliptical orbits
speed and slow time.

Love is also not cast,
but it *can* be tested until it dies.
When one begins to orbit
a new heavenly body,
creating distance, and is pulled
by that source of gravity,
when the altitude from walking on air
distorts time—slowing when far away,
and speeding when near—
and one has to leave for a landing
back home where the heart no longer spins,
and the equator bulges,
this distorted path fails to hold the course,
then love is no longer an *ever-fixed mark.*

Hiding the Chick

When your head is turned away from me,
I ease the small resin chick out of its perch
on the *Game of Thrones* bookend
near the yellow lighted lamp.
It has been hidden in full-view for two days
now. It's time to move it and start the next round
of hide-and-seek. You go about your business
killing one monster after another with one
mighty smote here, and a full-out battle there.
My chance opens as your character dies
and you close your eyes in defeat. The chick
is easily set next to you on the end table
as I plant a kiss on the crown of your head
which is in slight need of some trimming:
the stray hairs tickle my nose. I wonder
how long it will take for you to find the chick
and move it to a new and silly location
like the time I found the chick near the toaster
holding a metal knife: my favorite.

Your playfulness attracts me, making life
fun, youthful in my late seasons, so I
sit next to you on the plaid couch
as idle as I can be enjoying your gaming skills.
A few hours pass, and I discover you
have somehow sneaked past me
during the afternoon and wrapped the chick
in toilet paper like a sleeping bag,
and with characteristic
consideration have folded yet more
into a pillow to cushion its tiny head,
and placed it on the bathroom vanity

just so.

Paring it Down

The peel hangs from the tip of the knife—
one long curlicue of red and green—
over the gaping maw of the disposal
about to be fed. The paring drops into the abyss,
which eats greedily with one flick of the wall switch.
The knife now cuts through the apple pulp,
making four large fresh chunks
he sets in a red bowl after removing the stem,
core and pips.

It's routine before settling into the recliner—
brown and stuffed near the fireplace—
to watch TV at the end of a long day
of healthy choices intended to clean excess sugars
from his blood. He plans to stay with me
many more years and I watch his fist
rise to his mouth as he looks at me—
his fingers push the fruit
between his smiling lips.

Maturity

The radio is tuned to the Beatles station:
we listen to history, anecdotes, the poetry,
the beat. I return to the first forays
of my youth, to kisses beyond the campfire's edge
where the light is faint enough
to hide fear, but bright enough to shine
into open eyes that should be closed.
When it isn't love—I learned—the eyes
do not close. They don't sweep the light
under the lashes and lids where the brain
takes over telling the heart to pump
and skip and jump and settle down.

I'm glad to have not yet known you
in the experimental age that meant nothing,
even though now I am greedy
wanting to have had more time,
and to have yet more in the future
that years are stealing from us.

And I realize—oddly—that we entered our
union with eyes open wide.

Strawberry Fields Forever

The frost is thick upon my bedroom window pane,
and barely visible snowflakes
swirl, disappearing from my sight
then reappearing as I become winter.
I shiver a chill away, think of my lifetime friend
who lost her mother three days ago.
We were close in our youth. Warm memories
of lounging in hot summer gardens
eating cool, fresh strawberry pie
beneath Dutch elm branches punch today's ice.
She was close to her mother.
I want her to know that she, too, will be fine,
and will move forward as I have since my
mother died. I want to sit with her
again, and taste her mother's strawberry pie
perched on the window sill with summer sunshine
filtering through the dusty pane.

Today,
I will shop for a strawberry plant
to send her
even though it is Christmas
next week.

The Singing Bowl

Four months have passed, and I dust
the singing bowl once again.
With each swipe I recall your smile
when I agreed that I loved the bowl.
Christmas could not come soon enough
for you to *surprise* me.

The Japanese mark the passage of time
by sounding singing bowls. They honor
their dead by worshiping their ancestors,
meditating and healing
through sounding open bowls.

About the Author

Nancy Jo Allen was born and raised in Minneapolis, Minnesota, and now lives in Columbia, Missouri with her husband Terry and their pup Jayden. She earned her Master of Fine Arts in Writing (emphasis on playwriting) from Spalding University in Louisville, Kentucky. Her photos, fiction, and poetry are published in various journals included among them are *Well Versed,* *82 Review, Dime Show Review, Interpretations, Third Wednesday, Firewords, Common Ground, Down in the Dirt* and *I-70 Review.*

www.ingramcontent.com/pod-product-compliance
Lightning Source LLC
Chambersburg PA
CBHW031149090426
42738CB00008B/1273